COWHANDS AND CATTLE TRAILS

TABLE OF CONTENTS

by Margaret Moran

THE BEGINNING OF CATTLE TRAILS

The first cattle in North America came from Spain. The Spanish brought the cattle to Mexico when they settled there in the 1500s. These cattle were called **longhorns** because each of their horns could be up to three feet (91 centimeters) long. Their horns could also spread as wide as six feet (1.8 meters) across.

The cattle were not fenced in, and many strayed from their owners in search of grass and water. Over hundreds of years, some longhorns roamed as far north as Texas. The abundant grasslands on the Texas **plains** could feed many head of cattle. In time there were thousands, and then millions, of longhorn cattle in Texas.

The original Texas longhorns (top) were taller and thinner than modern Texas longhorns (right).

In the 1850s, Texas ranchers began rounding up some of these longhorns. They sold the cattle in New Orleans, Louisiana, and made large amounts of money. Although a large number of cattle were kept on ranches, about 2.9 million longhorns still roamed the **open range** in Texas in 1860.

Ranchers soon realized that there was more demand for beef in the rapidly growing cities of the East than there was in New Orleans. Meat-packing plants in Chicago supplied beef to the East. If ranchers could sell their herds to these plants, they could make fortunes. But how could they get their longhorns to Chicago?

▼ Before they could get a herd to market, ranchers had to put a herd together.

One meaning of the word "maverick" is an unbranded head of cattle. Samuel A. Maverick was a Texas cattleman in the 1840s and 1850s who did not brand his cattle.

Some ranchers tried driving their cattle north to railroads in Missouri, where the cattle could be loaded on railroad cars and shipped to Chicago. However, farmers along the way protested because Texas longhorns often carried a disease called Texas tick fever. The farmers did not want their cows infected. They also did not want their crops trampled by the traveling herds.

In addition, Missouri was quite far away, and the longhorns lost weight on their long walk. The less they weighed, the less they were worth to the meat-packers in Chicago.

A rope was, and still is, one of a cowhand's basic tools. ▼

THE ANNUAL ROUNDUP

Branding a cow took only seconds. ▲

There were no fences on the open range, so cattle could roam wherever they wanted. After the cows had their calves in the spring, ranchers had to sort out their herds. Several ranchers would get together and have a **roundup**. Their cowhands would ride out onto the range and find all the cattle in the area. Then the cowhands would drive the cattle to a central place.

The cows would all have been branded in earlier roundups. The cowhands would notice which calves belonged to which cows. The cowhands would rope the calves one at a time. Once a calf was roped and held down, it would be branded with the same **brand** as its mother. A cowhand would take a hot branding iron from the fire, and brand the calf. Then the calf would be released back to its mother. It only took a few minutes to rope and brand each calf, but there might be so many calves that a roundup would take a week or more.

THE CHISHOLM TRAIL

Joseph McCoy, an enterprising businessman, had a solution to the problem of getting Texas cattle to market more quickly and easily. He decided that a railroad line should be built somewhere on the Kansas plains. Kansas was ideal because it was closer to Texas than was Missouri. This meant that cattle drives would not have to be so long.

In 1867, McCoy convinced the Kansas Pacific Railroad to build a track from its main railroad line to the town of Abilene, Kansas. McCoy also helped extend the Chisholm Trail as far as Abilene.

The main street of Abilene was named Texas Street. It was the site of the Merchants Hotel. ▼

The Chisholm Trail started in San Antonio, Texas, and went through Oklahoma into Kansas. The trail was used by ranchers as a route for herding their cattle north.

McCoy approached several Kansas towns about building a **stockyard** to hold cattle waiting for shipment on the new railroad line. None were interested. Instead of giving up, McCoy bought the town of Abilene. He built his own stockyard to hold 3,000 head of cattle. He added a barn, an office for his business, and a hotel for the cowhands he knew would accompany the herds.

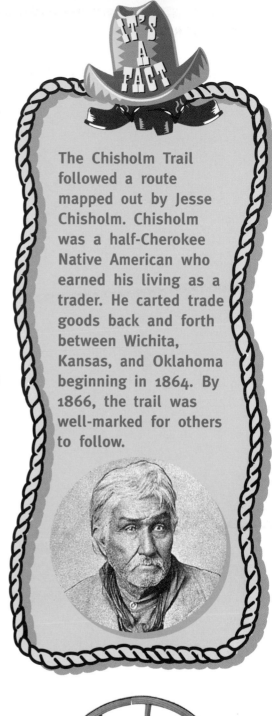

IT'S A FACT

The Chisholm Trail followed a route mapped out by Jesse Chisholm. Chisholm was a half-Cherokee Native American who earned his living as a trader. He carted trade goods back and forth between Wichita, Kansas, and Oklahoma beginning in 1864. By 1866, the trail was well-marked for others to follow.

Abilene would succeed only if someone would buy the herds that ranchers drove there. McCoy ran ads in Chicago newspapers to attract people who bought cattle for meat-packing plants. The ads announced Abilene's new stockyard and its link to the Kansas Pacific Railroad.

McCoy's work paid off in 1868. During that summer, more than 70,000 Texas longhorns came up the Chisholm Trail to the stockyard in Abilene.

In 1870, Texas ranchers drove about 300,000 longhorns to Abilene. Between 1867 and 1871, about 1.5 million longhorns passed through the stockyards of Abilene.

A head of cattle cost $5 in Texas, while the same cattle sold for $45 to $60 in Abilene. Some cattle ranchers made fortunes buying cheap cattle in Texas and selling them in Abilene at the higher price.

Several thousand cattle made up▶ each herd driven to Abilene.

Point

Reread

Reread pages 6–8 to identify the four most important ideas of the chapter.

LIFE ON A CATTLE DRIVE

To get their herds to Abilene, ranchers had to put together a **trail crew**. This was the men, horses, and equipment that moved the cattle along the trail.

Usually, a **trail herd** was made up of 1,500 to 3,000 head of cattle. For every 3,000 longhorns, a rancher sent a **trail boss**, 16 to 18 cowhands, a **wrangler**, a cook, and a cook's helper up the trail with the herd. The trail cook and his helper rode ahead of the herd and set up camp for the night.

The cowhands were called **drovers** because they drove, or guided, the cattle along. The wrangler took care of the drovers' horses. A cowhand didn't ride the same horse every day, so a trail crew of 18 men might have 150 horses.

Every cattle drive had its own trail crew. ◄

Cowhands called their food grub. Three times a day they ate beans, potatoes, biscuits, and coffee. Sometimes the crew killed a rabbit, deer, or stray steer. The cook whipped up a stew with the meat.

Mexican John was a famous trail cook. He figured out how to bake pies on a cattle drive.

Most drovers were young men. Often, the wrangler was a young boy. Drovers came from several different ethnic backgrounds. For example, about one in four drovers was African American. Many others were Mexican.

Trail crews had no tents. Each man slept wrapped up in a blanket on the ground, resting his head on his saddle. During the day, the cook carried the rolled-up blankets, known as bedrolls, in the chuckwagon. The chuckwagon also held changes of clothing for each drover.

Each member of the trail crew had a job. The leader was the trail boss. The trail boss often had several different jobs. He knew the trail the herd would follow, so he rode out ahead of the herd and looked for good campsites. He might be the manager of the ranch that was sending the cattle to market. He was responsible for selling the cattle when the herd arrived at the stockyards.

Although he was often just a boy, the wrangler had a very important job. The cowhands depended on him to provide fresh horses for them to ride every day. They spent 14 hours a day on horseback.

Cowhands might ride a thousand miles on a cattle drive. Sometimes their routes took them across wide rivers. ▼

At the front of the herd were two cowhands **riding point**. Riding point meant pointing, or steering, the herd in the right direction.

Many of the other cowhands were **riding swing**. Sometimes the herd stretched a mile long (1.6 kilometers) and 60 feet (18 meters) wide as it slowly walked north. The swing riders spaced themselves out on either side of the herd along its whole length. Their job was to keep the herd together and moving. Swing riders also went after any steers that tried to leave the herd.

At the end of the line of cattle were three cowhands **riding drag**. Their job was to keep the weak and slower cattle moving. Riding drag was a dusty job.

THE COMPLETE COWHAND

The Western saddle had a high saddle horn for a cowhand to hold onto when getting on and off his horse.

The cowhand tied one end of his rope to the saddle horn to hold it after he roped a steer.

A cowhand used the stirrups to get on and off a horse, as well as to stay on the horse.

Boots had pointed toes and high heels. The pointed toe made it easier for the cowhand to get his foot into the stirrup. The heel helped keep the foot in the stirrup.

A big Stetson hat protected the cowhand's head from sun, snow, and rain.

The bandana had many uses. It could protect the cowhand's neck from the sun and his face from dust. He could use it as a towel and as a bandage.

The rope was also called a lariat. The cowhand always had a lariat tied to the side of his saddle.

Levi® jeans were made of material that was tough and long-lasting.

Chaps were leather leggings worn over the cowhand's jeans. They protected his legs as he rode.

Cowhands used spurs to make their horses run faster.

15

A **stampede** was always a danger on a cattle drive. Cattle are nervous, and cattle in a large herd are even more nervous. Most stampedes happened at night when the herd had stopped. A loud noise—such as a shout or a gunshot—could set off a stampede. The most common causes were thunder and lightning.

A sharp crack of lightning or a crashing clap of thunder could unsettle a herd of cattle. Most would run in the same direction, but some would run off on their own. This created extra work for the cowhands.

IT'S A FACT

Cowhands sang to the cattle at night to calm them. The steady rhythm of the song lulled the cattle. These are two of the songs they sang.

"The Old Chisholm Trail"

Come along, boys,
and listen to my tale,

I'll tell you of my troubles
on the old Chisholm Trail.

(Chorus)

Coma ti yi youpy, youpy yea,
youpy yea,

Coma ti yi youpy, youpy yea.

"Home on the Range"

(Chorus)

Oh, give me a home,

Where the buffalo roam,

Where the deer
and the antelope play;

Where seldom is heard
a discouraging word,

And the skies are not
cloudy all day.

To stop a stampede, the cowhands would ride right into the middle of the herd. The men and horses would slowly get the herd to move in a giant circle. The cowhands would push the cattle toward the center of the circle. As the herd went around and around, the cowhands would continue to push the cattle together. As the cattle began to bunch up, they slowed down. The cattle would continue to run around in a circle that got smaller and smaller. Finally, the circle got so small that the cattle could not move. They had to stop. This is what "running around in a circle" means. It means going nowhere.

Point

Picture This
Reread pages 16–17. Close your eyes and picture the author's words. What do you see?

Thunder and lightning were sure to stampede a herd.
▼

A cattle drive up the Chisholm Trail took two to three months. The herd and the trail horses walked about 1,000 miles before they reached the stockyard in Abilene. When the herd got to Abilene, the trail boss and the cattle buyers argued about what the herd was worth. The trail boss sold the herd to the buyer who offered the highest price.

The drovers then led the herd into pens in the stockyard. The cattle were held there until a train came through to take them away.

Cattle towns weren't much to look at. But drovers were happy to spend time in them before getting on a horse again. ▼

Once the herd was sold, the trail boss paid the cowhands. They received from $25 to $40 a month for a cattle drive. That would be about $275 to $440 today. How much money each cowhand got depended on experience. Newer drovers received less money than more experienced ones.

Some cowhands spent much of their pay right in Abilene. They often drank and gambled their money away and rode back to Texas broke.

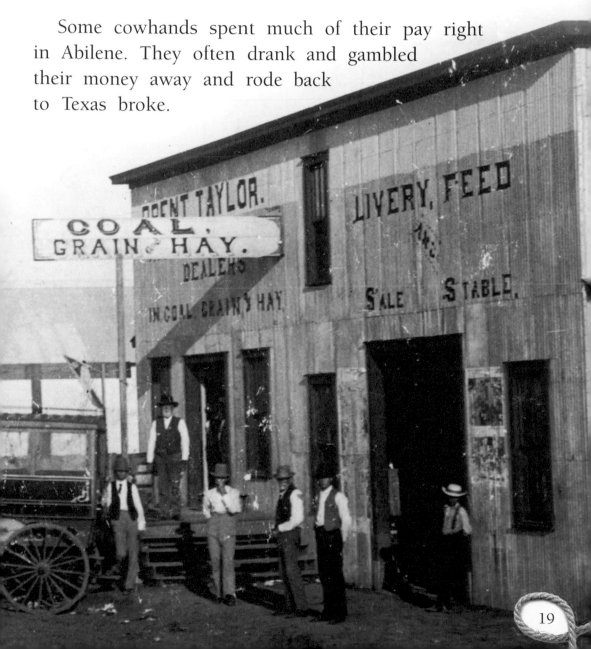

THE GOODNIGHT-LOVING TRAIL

In the 1870s, Abilene became less important as a railroad link for shipping cattle. Other towns farther west—such as Dodge City, Kansas—took its place. New trails reached these towns from Texas, and the Chisholm Trail became less traveled.

The map on the next page shows some of these trails. Not all of them ended at railroads. Some, like the Goodnight-Loving Trail, went as far as Cheyenne, Wyoming. The ranchers who sent their herds along these trails had found new markets for their cattle.

These cattle ranchers sold their cattle to people other than buyers for meat-packing plants in Chicago and other midwestern cities. They sold their cattle to the United States government. Texas ranchers also sold their herds to ranchers on the northern **Great Plains** so they could raise cattle for a living.

GUIDE MAP
OF THE
GREAT
Texas Cattle Trail
FROM
RED RIVER CROSSING
TO THE
OLD RELIABLE
KANSAS PACIFIC RAILWAY.

Published by the
Kansas Pacific Railway Co. for Gratuitous Distribution.
1875.

▲ Guide maps, usually published by railroad companies, helped cowhands move their herds to the stockyards.

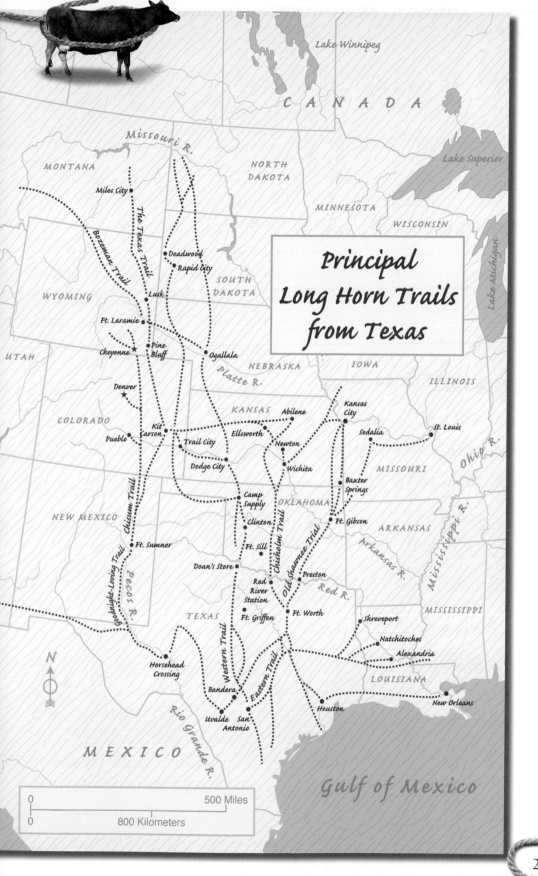

Lake Winnipeg

C A N A D A

Lake Superior

Missouri R.

MONTANA

NORTH
DAKOTA

MINNESOTA

WISCONSIN

Miles City

Lake Michigan

The Texas Trail

Bozeman Trail

WYOMING

Deadwood
Rapid City

SOUTH
DAKOTA

Lusk

Ft. Laramie

Principal
Long Horn Trails
from Texas

Cheyenne
Pine
Bluff

Ogallala

Platte R.

NEBRASKA

IOWA

ILLINOIS

UTAH

Denver

COLORADO

Kit
Carson

Pueblo

Trail City

Dodge City

Ellsworth

KANSAS

Abilene

Newton

Wichita

Kansas
City

Sedalia

St. Louis

Ohio R.

MISSOURI

Chisum Trail

NEW MEXICO

Goodnight-Loving Trail

Ft. Sumner

Camp
Supply

Clinton

Ft. Sill

OKLAHOMA

Baxter
Springs

Ft. Gibson

ARKANSAS

Arkansas R.

Mississippi R.

Pecos R.

Doan's Store

Red
River
Station

Preston

Old Shawnee Trail

Chisholm Trail

Red R.

MISSISSIPPI

TEXAS

Ft. Griffen

Ft. Worth

Shreveport

Natchitoches

Western Trail

Horsehead
Crossing

Eastern Trail

Alexandria

LOUISIANA

Bandera

Rio Grande R.

Uvalde

San
Antonio

Houston

New Orleans

M E X I C O

N

Gulf of Mexico

0   500 Miles
0   800 Kilometers

21

The Goodnight-Loving Trail was named after Charles Goodnight and Oliver Loving. They were both cattle ranchers. In 1866, the two men joined their herds and mapped a new trail to a new market.

The trail began in Fort Worth, Texas, went west to Fort Sumner, New Mexico, and then north to Colorado. Goodnight and Loving sold part of their herd to the army in New Mexico. The army used the cattle to feed soldiers and Native Americans on reservations. Goodnight and Loving sold the rest of the cattle as food to miners in Colorado.

In 1868, Goodnight took a herd of cattle all the way to Cheyenne, Wyoming. A Wyoming rancher bought those cattle to stock his ranch.

IT'S A FACT

Charles Goodnight did more than lay out the Goodnight-Loving Trail. He also designed the chuckwagon. It was his idea to make a wooden box at the back of the wagon. When opened, the front of the box came down like a table. The cook used it for work space. Goodnight called this a chuckbox. Soon other trail crews were using Goodnight's design for the chuckbox.

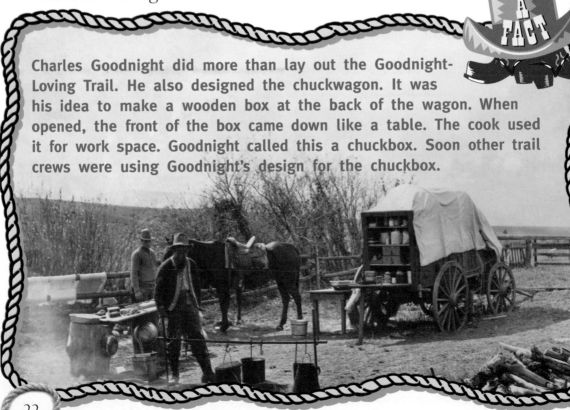

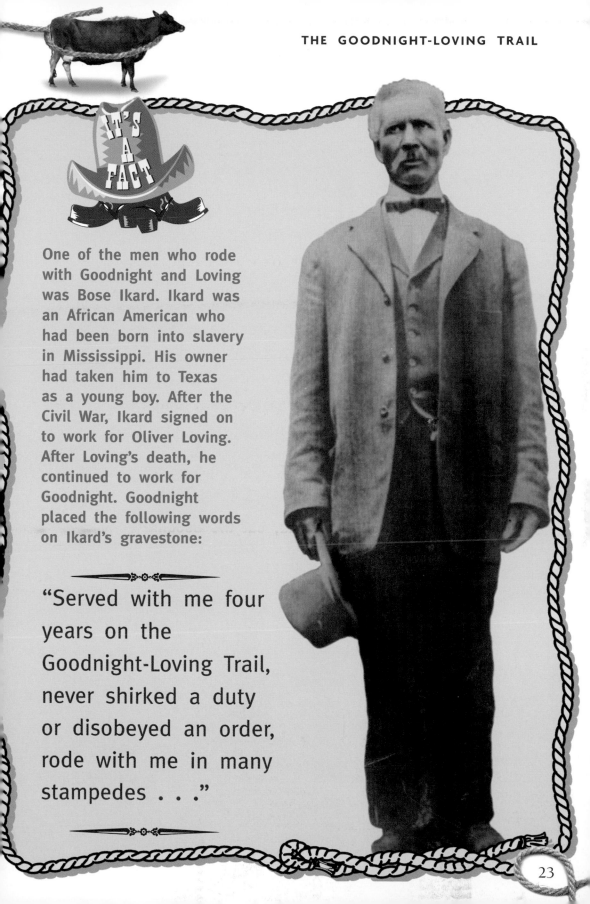

One of the men who rode with Goodnight and Loving was Bose Ikard. Ikard was an African American who had been born into slavery in Mississippi. His owner had taken him to Texas as a young boy. After the Civil War, Ikard signed on to work for Oliver Loving. After Loving's death, he continued to work for Goodnight. Goodnight placed the following words on Ikard's gravestone:

"Served with me four years on the Goodnight-Loving Trail, never shirked a duty or disobeyed an order, rode with me in many stampedes . . ."

THE END OF THE CATTLE DRIVES

IT'S A FACT

The twisted pieces of wire are called barbs. At first ranchers wouldn't buy barbed wire for fencing. They thought it would hurt their cattle. The inventor, Joseph Glidden, had to prove that this was not true. He had a barbed wire corral built and put steers in it. The ranchers soon saw that cattle did not get stuck on the barbs.

By 1890, the days of the long Texas cattle drives were over. Several things caused their end.

First, the number of railroad lines increased. Some railroads began to lay track in Texas closer to the herds. Ranchers no longer had to drive their herds to Kansas or farther north to sell them.

Second, the open range started to become fenced in when barbed wire was invented in 1874. The first Texas longhorns had roamed freely on the plains. Ranchers needed only to rope and brand them to gather a herd.

◀ The sharp points on the barbed wire kept the cattle from trampling it.

✔ Point

Think It Over

Compare this picture of a farm family with the picture of the drovers on pages 10–11. How were their lives the same? Different?

But now ranchers with big ranches fenced in their land with barbed wire, which was cheap and easy to install. A cowhand still had to dig the holes for fence posts, but he didn't have to saw pieces of wood and nail them onto the posts. He just had to nail the barbed wire between the posts. Using the barbed wire, these ranchers could keep their cattle on their ranches, and other cattle out. Farmers and sheep ranchers also used barbed wire to keep cattle off their property and away from their water and grass.

No longer could cattle roam freely in search of grass and water. Fencing the range hurt ranchers who had small ranches. Their land did not have enough grass and water to feed their herds. Fencing made it impossible for the small ranchers to get their herds to grassland and water.

Third, two bad winters and a bad summer killed millions of cattle. During the winter of 1885–1886, blizzards and temperatures far below zero hit the Great Plains and killed many cattle. A drought in the summer of 1886 left the plains brown and dry. More cattle died because of a lack of water.

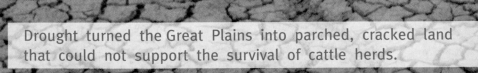

Drought turned the Great Plains into parched, cracked land that could not support the survival of cattle herds.

The following year, more freezing cold and blizzards left the plains covered with dead cattle. Some ranchers never recovered from the loss of so many cattle.

Fourth, the price of beef dropped sharply. Cattle ranchers could no longer make a living by raising cattle.

Between 1885 and 1888, millions of head of cattle starved or froze to death on the Great Plains. This modern-day cattle drive is taking place in snowy, but not deadly, conditions.

CONCLUSION

The golden age of cattle drives lasted only 28 years—from 1860 to 1888. It was an exciting time in United States history.

1860

Some 2.9 million longhorns roam the open range in Texas.

1865

Meat-packing plants in Chicago supply beef to the East. If ranchers could sell their herds to these plants, they could make fortunes.

1862

Joseph McCoy's cattle town of Abilene opens for business.

1864

Jesse Chisholm begins carting trade goods back and forth between Wichita, Kansas, and Oklahoma.

1866

The Chisholm Trail is well marked for others to follow.

1866-1868

The Goodnight-Loving trail is laid out to Colorado, and then to Wyoming.

1860

1870

1868

More than 70,000 head of cattle pass through the stockyard at Abilene.

1885-1886

Winter blizzards and temperatures far below zero hit the Great Plains, killing thousands of cattle.

1886

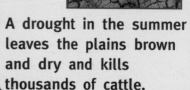

A drought in the summer leaves the plains brown and dry and kills thousands of cattle.

1870

Texas ranchers drive 300,000 longhorns to Abilene.

1887-1888

Another winter of freezing cold and blizzards leaves the plains covered with more dead cattle.

1874

Some 2.9 million longhorns roam the open range in Texas.

1880

1890

Point

Think It Over

People today still find the life of a cattle rancher attractive. Many dude ranches offer the opportunity for people to experience a bit of this life. Would you have enjoyed being a cattle rancher? Why or why not?

SOUTHWESTERN
Dude Ranches

Santa Fe

GLOSSARY

brand	(BRAND) a mark on a head of cattle showing which ranch owns it (page 5)
drover	(DROH-ver) a cowhand (page 10)
Great Plains	(GRAYT PLAYNS) huge area of flat land extending across the center of the United States from north to south and east to west (page 20)
longhorn	(LAHNG-horn) cow with very long horns that can be up to three feet in length (page 2)
open range	(OH-pen RAYNJ) unfenced grassland across the U.S. West (page 3)
plains	(PLAYNS) flat, mostly treeless grasslands (page 2)
riding drag	(RIGHD-eeng DRAG) to ride at the back of a herd on a cattle drive to keep it moving (page 13)
riding point	(RIGHD-eeng POYNT) to ride out in front of a herd on a cattle drive; to lead it (page 13)
riding swing	(RIGHD-eeng SWING) to ride on either side of a herd on a cattle drive to keep the herd moving forward (page 13)
roundup	(ROWND-uhp) the gathering of cattle into place for branding calves (page 5)
stampede	(stam-PEED) the running away of cattle in all directions (page 16)
stockyard	(STAHK-yahrd) the place where cattle are kept before shipment by railroad (page 7)
trail boss	(TRAYL BAHS) the leader of a cattle drive (page 10)
trail crew	(TRAYL KROO) the men, horses, and equipment that moved cattle along the trail (page 10)
trail herd	(TRAYL HERD) 1,500 to 3,000 head of cattle (page 10)
wrangler	(WRAYNG-ler) the person who takes care of horses (page 10)

INDEX